GRAPHIC DINOSAURS

IGUANODON

IGUANA TOOTH

BY DAVID WEST

PowerKiDS press.
New York

Published in 2012 by The Rosen Publishing Group, Inc.
29 East 21st Street, New York 10010

Designed and produced by
David West Books

Designed and written by David West

Library of Congress Cataloging-in-Publication Data

West, David (David William), 1956–
Iguanodon : iguana tooth / By David West.
pages cm. — (Graphic Dinosaurs)
Includes index.
ISBN 978-1-4488-5205-5 (library binding) — ISBN 978-1-4488-5248-2 (pbk.)
— ISBN 978-1-4488-5249-9 (6-pack)
1. Iguanodon—Juvenile literature. I. Title.
QE862.O65W443 2012
567.914—dc22

2010048987

Manufactured in China

CPSIA Compliance Information: Batch #DS1102PK:
For Further Information contact Rosen Publishing, New York,
New York at 1-800-237-9932

CONTENTS

WHAT IS AN IGUANODON?

IGUANODON MEANS "IGUANA TOOTH."

Its toothless beak was used to feed on plants.

Its long tail helped it balance while walking on two legs.

Its long arms with strong padded hands meant it could walk on four limbs as well as two.

Large thumb spikes were used as a defense and for feeding.

Its little finger was used to grasp twigs and leaves while it was feeding.

IGUANODON LIVED AROUND 140 TO 110 MILLION YEARS AGO, DURING THE **LOWER CRETACEOUS PERIOD. FOSSILS** OF ITS SKELETON HAVE BEEN FOUND IN BELGIUM, ENGLAND, GERMANY, SPAIN, AND THE UNITED STATES (SEE PAGE 30).

Adult Iguanodons measured up to 36 feet (11 m) long and weighed about 6 tons (5 t).

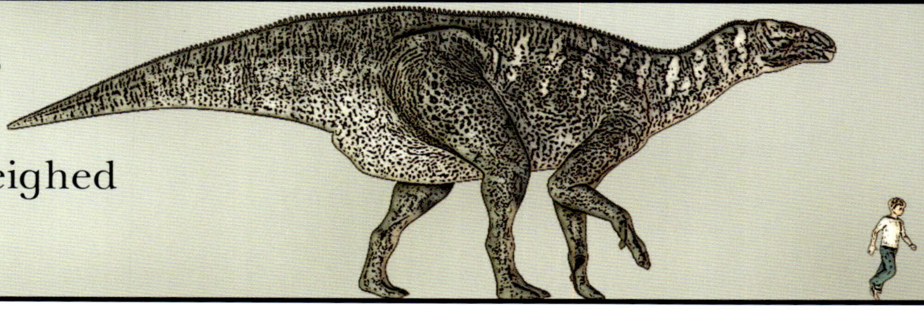

PLANT EATER

Iguanodon had rows of grinding teeth similar to those of an iguana but much bigger. It used its beak to tear off pieces from a plant and it would then munch on these with its rows of teeth.

Iguanodon's fossilized skull

MULTIPURPOSE HANDS

Iguanodon had the most unusual hands of any animal. They had blunt hooves, which meant they probably walked on all fours some of the time and probably could gallop for short distances. They also had a sharp thumb spike. **Paleontologists** think these were used as a defense against **predators** and also to help dislodge plant matter. The little finger on each hand was used to hold on to plants while feeding.

Fossilized hand bones of Iguanodon

HERDS

Fossils of many Iguanodons have been found together. This suggests that these animals lived in herds like modern buffalo.

A herd of African buffalo

PART ONE... ESCAPE!

WITHOUT WARNING, A TREE CRASHES DOWN A SHORT DISTANCE FROM THE JUVENILE. THE YOUNG IGUANODON LETS OUT A SHOCKED BELLOW.
CRASH
BWAAAR
OTHER MEMBERS OF THE HERD LOOK UP AND CALL OUT IN ALARM.
GRAAAR
GRAAAR
BWAAAR
THE HERD SETTLES DOWN AS THEY REALIZE IT IS ONLY A PELOROSAURUS. IT HAS PUSHED THE TREE DOWN SO THAT IT CAN FEED ON THE BRANCHES IT COULD NOT REACH.

SUDDENLY THERE IS A LOUD BANG FOLLOWED BY A ROARING NOISE. LOOKING UP, THE DINOSAURS SEE THAT THE TOP OF THE VOLCANO HAS EXPLODED.
KABOOM

LARGE FIERY BOMBS OF MOLTEN ROCK BEGIN TO RAIN DOWN ON THE DINOSAURS.

THE HERD OF IGUANODONS RUNS IN PANIC AWAY FROM THE VOLCANO, WHICH IS SPITTING FIRE AND SMOKE IN EVERY DIRECTION.

THE JUVENILE FOLLOWS THE HERD. HE IS OVERTAKEN BY THE ARISTOSUCHUSES THAT HAD BEEN STALKING HIM. THEY ARE NOW RUNNING FOR THEIR LIVES.

A SMOKING LAVA BOMB HITS THE PELOROSAURUS, AND IT LETS OUT A ROAR OF PAIN.
BRAAAWR

THE DINOSAURS RUN FOR THEIR LIVES AS FIRES BREAK OUT AMONG THE DRY VEGETATION ON THE VALLEY FLOOR.
THE SMOKE GETS THICKER, AND THE JUVENILE LOSES SIGHT OF HIS HERD.
COUGH
HE STUMBLES ON, CHOKING ON THE THICK SMOKE.

UNABLE TO SEE PROPERLY, THE JUVENILE JOINS A GROUP OF DINOSAURS MOVING IN THE SAME DIRECTION. HE WANTS THEIR PROTECTION.

AS THE SMOKE CLEARS HE SUDDENLY BECOMES AWARE THAT HE IS FOLLOWING A GROUP OF NEOVENATORS. THESE LARGE KILLERS PREY ON HIS KIND.

LUCKILY, THEY HAVEN'T NOTICED HIM. HE STOPS AND CROUCHES BEHIND A ROCK AND WAITS FOR THEM TO DISAPPEAR FROM SIGHT.

PART TWO... LOST!

THE NEXT DAY, THE YOUNG IGUANODON CONTINUES TO LOOK FOR HIS HERD. HE WALKS ALONG A LONG BEACH. THERE IS A THICK MIST, WHICH ALLOWS HIM TO SEE ONLY A SHORT DISTANCE.

THE JUVENILE PANICS AND RUNS FOR HIS LIFE. HE FINDS HIMSELF CLOSE TO THE WALL OF A CLIFF.
SUDDENLY A DARK OPENING APPEARS, AND HE RUNS INTO A CAVE.
THE NEOVENATORS PASS BY.
HE FEELS SAFER IN THE CAVE. BUT THEN SOMETHING MAKES A NOISE IN THE DARKNESS.
UGH UGH

THERE IS A SHUFFLING SOUND AS THE ANIMAL MOVES TOWARD THE JUVENILE, WHO IS FROZEN WITH FEAR.

OUT OF THE GLOOM APPEARS WHAT LOOKS LIKE A SMALL IGUANODON. IT IS A VALDOSAURUS, A TYPE OF IGUANODONT.
GRAARK
IT RECOGNIZES THE SHAPE OF THE IGUANODON AND THINKS HE IS FROM THE SAME FAMILY. IT MOVES CLOSER FOR PROTECTION.

THE IGUANODON PEERS OUT FROM THE CAVE. THE MIST HAS DISAPPEARED AND THE NEOVENATORS CAN BE SEEN FEEDING ON THE CARCASS OF THE INJURED PELOROSAURUS.

THE IGUANODON LEAVES THE CAVE AND HEADS UP THE COAST, AWAY FROM THE FEEDING MEAT EATERS. HE IS FOLLOWED BY THE VALDOSAURUS.

THE YOUNG IGUANODON ARRIVES AT A LARGE **ESTUARY**. ON THE OTHER SIDE HE CAN SEE HIS HERD FEEDING ON PLANTS. THEY CROSSED EARLIER IN THE DAY, WHEN THE TIDE WAS OUT AND IT WAS SHALLOWER.
BRAAARRR
THE JUVENILE WALKS INTO THE WATER. HE IS DESPERATE TO JOIN HIS HERD. THE VALDOSAURUS FOLLOWS HIM.
THE INCOMING TIDE IS STRONG. SUDDENLY BOTH DINOSAURS ARE SWEPT AWAY.
BLAA
MAAHH

THE DINOSAURS TRY TO KEEP THEIR HEADS ABOVE THE SURFACE OF THE WATER.
GRAARRRK

FINALLY THEY MAKE IT TO THE RIVER'S EDGE AND DRAG THEMSELVES UP THE BANK.

PART THREE...
DANGER!
THE TWO DINOSAURS HAVE LANDED ON THE WRONG SIDE OF THE RIVER AND STILL NEED TO CROSS OVER. AS THEY WALK ALONG THE RIVERBANK THEY DISCOVER THAT THEY ARE NOT OUT OF DANGER.
A LARGE MEAT-EATING DINOSAUR IS HEADING THEIR WAY.
IT IS A BARYONYX AND IT PREYS ON MANY ANIMALS, INCLUDING IGUANODONTS.

THE TWO IGUANODONTS FREEZE. THERE IS NO WAY TO ESCAPE EXCEPT BACK INTO THE DANGEROUS RIVER. THE BARYONYX IS ALMOST ON THEM.
GRRRR

SUDDENLY IT STOPS. IT HAS SEEN SOMETHING.

THE BARYONYX LEAPS INTO THE RIVER.

LUCKILY FOR THE IGUANODONTS, THE BARYONYX LIKES TO FEED ON FISH. IT GRABS HOLD OF A LARGE FISH, WHICH WRIGGLES OUT OF ITS GRASP.

THE BARYONYX CHASES AFTER THE INJURED FISH INTO DEEPER WATER.

THE BARYONYX DISAPPEARS DOWN THE RIVER. THE TWO IGUANODONTS CONTINUE ALONG THE RIVERBANK, LOOKING FOR A PLACE TO CROSS.

AS THEY ROUND A BEND IN THE RIVER THEY COME TO A SHALLOW CROSSING POINT, WHERE A GROUP OF POLACANTHUSES ARE DRINKING AT THE RIVER'S EDGE.

SUDDENLY A PAIR OF HYPSILOPHODONS COME RUSHING OUT OF THE UNDERGROWTH. THEY ARE CALLING AN ALARM.
GRAAARK
GRAAARK
THEY ARE FOLLOWED BY A LARGE, HUNGRY EOTYRANNUS.
GRAAARRGH

THE POLACANTHUSES HAVE BEEN WARNED BY THE HYPSILOPHODONS, AND THEY FORM A DEFENSIVE WALL OF SPIKED ARMOR.
RAAARRGH

THE EOTYRANNUS IS PUT OFF BY THE ARMORED WALL. AFTER ROARING A FEW TIMES, IT TURNS AND SLOWLY WALKS AWAY.

FINALLY THE POLACANTHUSES SETTLE DOWN AND START FEEDING, AND THE TWO IGUANODONTS CROSS THE RIVER.

PART FOUR...
SAFE!
THE TWO IGUANODONTS STOP TO FEED WITH THE POLACANTHUSES. THEY HAVE NOT EATEN SINCE THE VOLCANO ERUPTED A DAY AND A HALF AGO.

A GROWLING SOUND FROM DOWNSTREAM ALERTS THE FEEDING DINOSAURS TO THE RETURNING BARYONYX.
GRRRRRR

THEY ALL MOVE QUICKLY INTO THE FOREST.

THE TWO IGUANODONTS SOON FIND THEMSELVES WALKING ACROSS A DESERT. OVERHEAD, AN ORNITHOCHEIRUS GLIDES SOUTH TOWARD THE COAST. THE JUVENILE IS HEADING IN THE SAME DIRECTION, HOPING TO JOIN HIS HERD.
AARRK

UNKNOWN TO THE TWO IGUANODONTS, THE EOTYRANNUS HAS SPOTTED THEM FROM HIGH UP ON A CLIFF.
GRRRRRR

IT TAKES TIME FOR THE EOTYRANNUS TO FIND A WAY DOWN TO THE DESERT FLOOR.

FINALLY IT GETS TO THE GROUND AND SETS OFF AFTER THE TWO IGUANODONTS.

THE IGUANODONTS REACH A STEEP SLOPE. IT SEEMS TOO DANGEROUS TO WALK DOWN.

AS THEY TURN AROUND THEY SEE THE EOTYRANNUS CHARGING TOWARD THEM.

THE TWO IGUANODONTS TURN IN TERROR AND HEAD DOWN THE SLOPE AT A GALLOP.
AARRK

THE SLOPE IS TOO STEEP FOR THE IGUANODONTS, AND THEY LOSE THEIR FOOTING.
WAAARGH
GRAAARGH
THE EOTYRANNUS IS CLOSE BEHIND.
THE TWO IGUANODONTS FALL TO THE BOTTOM OF THE SLOPE.
THE EOTYRANNUS STOPS SUDDENLY. IT IS LOOKING AT SOMETHING BEYOND THE TWO IGUANODONTS.

FOUR VERY LARGE MALE IGUANODONS ARE REARING UP ON THEIR HIND LEGS, DISPLAYING THEIR SHARP THUMB SPIKES.

THE EOTYRANNUS BACKS OFF. IT WILL NOT RISK GETTING INJURED AND WALKS AWAY FROM THE YOUNG IGUANODONTS.

THE PLAIN IS DOTTED WITH MANY HERDS OF DINOSAURS, INCLUDING THE JUVENILE'S OWN HERD. HE HAS FINALLY MADE IT TO THE SAFETY AND PROTECTION OF HIS OWN KIND. THEY DON'T EVEN MIND HAVING THE SMALL VALDOSAURUS JOIN THEM.

FOSSIL EVIDENCE

WE CAN GET A GOOD IDEA OF WHAT DINOSAURS MAY HAVE LOOKED LIKE FROM THEIR FOSSILS. FOSSILS ARE FORMED WHEN THE HARD PARTS OF AN ANIMAL OR PLANT ARE BURIED AND THEN TURN TO ROCK OVER MILLIONS OF YEARS.

Iguanodon was the second dinosaur ever to be named and the first dinosaur to be recognized for what it really was. Iguanodon was discovered 20 years before the word “dinosaur” was ever used. After discovering some fossilized teeth in Sussex, England, in 1822, Gideon Mantell was determined to find out which animal they had belonged to. After several years he discovered they were similar to an iguana’s teeth but much bigger. When a complete skeleton was found in 1834, it was possible to reconstruct what it might have looked like.

Early attempts at reconstruction had the thumb spike placed on its nose as a horn. In 1878, at least 38 Iguanodon fossils were discovered in a coal mine at Bernissart in Belgium, suggesting that they lived in herds.

An early reconstruction of Iguanodon

Reconstructing a Bernissart fossil

ANIMAL GALLERY

ALL THESE ANIMALS APPEAR IN THE STORY.

Aristosuchus
"Noble crocodile"
Length: 6.5 ft (2 m)
A two-legged, meat-eating theropod dinosaur.

Hypsilophodon
"High-ridge tooth"
Length: 6.5 ft (2 m)
A two-legged, plant-eating ornithopod dinosaur.

Valdosaurus
"Wealden lizard"
Length: 10 ft (3 m)
A two-legged, plant-eating ornithopod dinosaur.

Polacanthus
"Many spines"
Length: 16 ft (5 m)
An armored, spiked, plant-eating ankylosaur.

Eotyrannus
"Dawn tyrant"
Length: 20 ft (6 m)
A meat-eating theropod dinosaur.

Neovenator
"New hunter"
Length: 25 ft (7.5 m)
A meat-eating allosauroid dinosaur.

Baryonyx
"Heavy claw"
Length: 33 ft (10 m)
A large, meat- and fish-eating dinosaur.

Ornithocheirus
"Bird hand"
Wingspan: 39 ft (12 m)
A large flying reptile.

Pelorosaurus
"Monstrous lizard"
Length: 82 ft (25 m)
A giant, long-necked, plant-eating dinosaur.

GLOSSARY

carcass (KAR-kus) The body of a dead animal.

cycads (SY-kudz) Fernlike evergreen plants that have short, fat trunks.

estuary (ES-choo-wer-ee) An area of water where a river runs into the sea.

fossils (FO-sulz) The remains of living things that have turned to rock.

iguanodonts (i-GWAH-nuh-donts) Plant-eating dinosaurs, which included duckbills, that lived from the Mid-Jurassic to Late Cretaceous periods.

juvenile (JOO-vuh-nyl) A young animal that is not fully grown.

Lower Cretaceous period (LOH-er krih-TAY-shus PIR-ee-ud) The period of time between 145 and 98 million years ago.

paleontologists (pay-lee-on-TO-luh-jists) Scientists who study fossils.

predators (PRE-duh-terz) Animals that hunt animals.

INDEX

Web Sites
Due to the changing nature of Internet links, The Rosen Publishing Group, Inc., has developed an online list of Web sites related to the subject of this book. This site is updated regularly. Please use this link to access the list:
www.powerkidslinks.com/gdino/iguan/